C000049472

Strange Husbandry

Through pandemic isolation and upheaval; through the glitter and gutters of London; through spectral exes and specular new love; through the guts of night, the self, Tori Amos, and the moon, *Strange Husbandry* sings. This is a book that won't stop singing and you won't be able to stop listening. What stirring, truth-bringing sounds–and imagery that vibrates, resonates as the most aching music, too: "for I am the Love, your Dog. / I am a mouthful of such sweet god–"These poems inhabit a visceral vertigo–right before a swift, plunging descent—and they somehow inhabit that fall, too. By turns thrilling and terrifying, sensual and celestial, Lorcán Black's work will leave you not wanting to leave its dictions, its frictions, its worlds with "everything drooping and leaking, / hanging/heavy/heavenly."
– Chen Chen, author of *When I Grow Up I Want to Be a List of Further Possbilities and Your Emergency Contact Has Experienced An Emergency.*

Lorcán Black's much-anticipated second collection, *Strange Husbandry*, gathers together a symphony of voices–iconic figures of history, mythology, religion—to offer insight into human pain and wonder. Against the backdrop of the past, Black considers the present–illness, war, and whatever love we can find here. These urgent poems are warnings, confessions, declarations, and blessings. I feel them, sensorial and lyric, within my own body.
– Blas Falconer, author of *Rara Avis* and *Forgive The Body This Failure*

Witnessing both the tragedy of contemporary events and their mythic counterparts, Lorcán Black's exquisitely rendered poems of sorcery and seduction move me with their imagistic sense of wonder, all the while being fully attuned to a world that is 'steadily uncertain.' *Strange Husbandry* is a collection alert to beauty and to terror.
– Richie Hofmann, author of *100 Lovers* and *Second Empire*

"Strange Husbandry" is the "contagious fever of a whole hot hive." In Black's poems, "every man looked like danger." The mystical narrative collection explores trauma trapped under the surface in the true stories of cultural icons. His poems "cut / straight through the heart of it: / this is the sacrifice." Love & beauty marries history & the subsequent fear here. The poems will leave or divorce you, like him, saying "I have never been so flush of blood".
– Crystal Stone, author of *All The Places I Wish I'd Died* and *White Lies*

Strange Husbandry is pure alchemy. It takes a handful of rubble, witnesses, its memory & pain, and then transforms it into something to be kept–placed into a museum where we, the reader, can return to it again and again to remind ourselves what we have overcome. Something new is happening here- something magical & made out of what has been lost. It's important that we take notice. Black is a poet whose name we will remember for a long time.
– Kailey Tedesco, author of *FOREVERHAUS, Lizzie, Speak* and *She Used to be on a Milk Carton*

Strange Husbandry

Lorcán Black

Seren is the book imprint of
Poetry Wales Press Ltd.
Suite 6, 4 Derwen Road, Bridgend,
Wales, CF31 1LH

www.serenbooks.com
Follow us on social media @SerenBooks

The right of Lorcán Black to be identified as
the author of this work has been asserted in accordance
with the Copyright, Designs and Patents Act, 1988.

© Lorcán Black, 2024.

ISBN: 978-1-78172-744-7
ebook: 978-1-78172-745-4

A CIP record for this title is available from the British Library.

All rights reserved. No part of this publication may be reproduced,
stored in a retrieval system, or transmitted at any time or by any means,
electronic, mechanical, photocopying, recording or otherwise without
the prior permission of the copyright holder.

The publisher acknowledges the financial assistance of the Books Council of Wales.

Cover painting: Martin Adalian, *Tarnished*.

Printed in Bembo by 4Edge Limited, Essex.

Dedicated to everyone I love
who thinks 'Is that about me?'

Yes. It is.

Stop doing things that make me
want to put you in poems.

'Strange': *definition*: Oxford English Dictionary:
1. Unusual or surprising; difficult to understand or explain.
E.G: *"children have some strange ideas"*

2. Not previously visited, seen, or encountered; unfamiliar or alien.
E.G: *"she was lost in a strange country"*

'Husbandry': *definition*: Oxford English Dictionary:
1. The care, cultivation, and breeding of crops and animals.
E.G: *"all aspects of animal husbandry"*

2. The management and conservation of resources, or one's means.
E.G: *"low borrowing demonstrates astute husbandry of resources"*

Contents

Aphrodite

The first train heaves & leaves,
rumbles & eats its track –
You turn to me,

> Sleep-eyed, docile & I know
> I have fifteen minutes of this.
> I watch your face, feel your beard grow.

I watch you wake
& very silently, very carefully,
one considers the other.

> Squirrelcall, birdcall, hands
> in chest hair –
> we grow branches, entangle –
> stiffen.

The whole morning
mornings out upon itself –

> a wave far off washes ashore.
> Over my belly a moon moves &
> a whole world, unseeing, senses oceans.

Surf catches itself in the wash
of its own white brilliance.
Was it an oyster shell she birthed from?

> Because he gifts me necklaces –
> all clear & salt like the sea
> of such bright, startling pearl

& these dropped pearls
my tongue, outstretching,
clutches –

Witch's Means

after the execution of Giles Corey, English colonialist accused of witchcraft in Salem, Massachusetts. 1692. Executed by being pressed to death by boulders.

Say I was a Swallowtail,
Apatura Iris or Inachis Io –
or any live specimen – because really,
what does it matter?
& you a scientist with your pins –
instead of inquisitor with your boulders –
cold metal points struck through
like pikes to the board beneath
as you stroke & stroke my pinned wings,
bands glittering in black, in gold,
in my fine-dusted ochre.

Pain is no object
& once pinned
you whisper to me of my own frail beauty –
how despite the pain & the pinning –
you love me, really, & how the Lord will set me free.
Even now, even like this:

pain-blind, froth-mouthed, seizing –
there is no stopping this.
How you love me more, pinned down,
how you love me still.

Inside, lamps are lit
white-bright. At the windows
moths gather, wings
shush glass unknowing
their small night-shadows
brush these beautiful brutalities.

Mullioned eyes seeing
only lightness, wonder,
white-glittered flame –
flinging themselves sick
& ecstatic as saints.

There is no getting up from this.

So let us pretend I am wingless & sightless.
So if I am wingless & sightless
it means: I become nothing more & nothing less.
Which means: I become nothing & everything.

Witch's means: I become all the night's dark spaces
& set myself to fly out
in a hush of wing-brushed night

& take my leave of that small voice,
wingless & sightless
gasping out

More weight,
more weight.

Nightswimming

Games of dominos in Portugal, whistling at girls
for laughs off the balcony –

Really, though, September was coming soon & here:
I thought you knew me –

those long nights on balconies:
my only infringement –

tussles in the sands:
sandals askew, sand in toes, sand-stuck,

those sunscreen, sea-washed days:
& a face so golden, so gold –

& where did you think I went:
those nights with boys?

Threshold

There will be no exchange of rings.
The years appear & vanish, easy as stars.
          A grim lightness has coalesced between us.

The long evenings billow out, we laugh
or are sullen – a threshold over which we lightly pass,
          steadily uncertain.

August

Here: the night's hot breath –
its own startling fright of silence,
or, in other words:

> the lack of your voice in blackness.
> Your sound in deep sleep –
> there are photographs.

Look: how the light drowns itself –
deep-shaded, darkening, the centre of dusk:
sundown, the suburbs,
wild vicissitudes.

Night –

> like a beloved lamp,
> smashed utterly, shaded over.

Lockdown

London 2021

Look
how quiet it is here –
how tight the night bites you.

These small mouths:
how teeth their sharp, small

movements at dawn/sleepless
flour-fingers rolling white dough
& milk churning over & over –

how we care to make a thing
beautiful enough
to bear.

How for days & days
there is a new cupcake/a cake/
something with folds/a softness –

anything sweet folded in on itself
like a baby/like a sweetness of faces/
families over a fence.

Spring months march heavy:
Summer/Winter –
& weight, like long still water,
like glass clouded over

& every morning
in the morning paper:
death in the news

Dawn birds crying/
strange choir,

like a host of swallows
      burning
      but flying over –

Hazmat

London 2020

The lungs of this city are burning.
Outside an ambulance expels three medics:

minutes later they move a man between them
like a chess piece.

From our terrace I see the thin, frail rage
of his chest rising & falling with each step.

The fever glowing – radiation hot –
chest heaving.

A woman stands by the door crying.
The suits help him tenderly:

three beekeepers carefully arranging
the contagious fever of a whole hot hive

to be hand delivered
into a white sterility.

Each night since I have stared at that house. What
if they ban funerals? What will she do but sit

memorising every detail: those men, eyes
under white hoods, escorting him off

into darkness? The sirens are silent.
Their lights disappear

into a night on fire with distance.
The spring trees are restless –

Listen –
their branches are breathing & creaking.

Tonight, & every night,
I can't help but think

what walls of what houses –
how many thousands are

caging grief, passing
mere time?

26 Charleville Mall

for Mary-Kate.

There is a lightbulb I'd promised to replace,
a tube of lipstick found in a drawer of a dresser.
Silk scarf draped on the bedroom floor

that same morning as though you'd come in
the evening before, shed it off
& let it slip through air

like a dry run.
I remember: a teacup abandoned,
milk curdling deep

in the swell of its belly –
why, when you felt suddenly ill,
you chose to die in the guest bedroom?

I thought it was so patient,
that cup. Like a dog –
sure you would come back to it.

How, when I'd tried to,
my shook, white hand failed
utterly to move it.

London Bridge Attack

The city is slick with rain.
I have been in a dream I dreamt
of a burrow of sorts/cars

with their heads cut off/of pain
pumping my legs onward,
breathless/escape-riddled:

hot metal flooding the clean
ivory of my teeth/& in the hot blood
the body/ I do not know

what any of this means.
I have bled you out/

somewhere there must be a
heart/blood – pumping
fatal, bruising/irrevocably

interminable.
Purple & black –
all inside an hour begging

how & how? & somewhere/
it feels like someone else
is breathing –

There is a bridge & the bridge
is wide: I cannot see
where I am to run to –

Hypatia

These are the things the Heavens turn on:
finality, its star-pricked black & silver air –

my scrolls dropped where they found me,
the streets paved in blood where they dragged me.

Rocks, stones, smashed slate.
Stripped & silk-shredded

they split the fruits of me open:
a bowl of sweet-juiced flesh –

my bones, my blood, my hair.
In the hot, close air of a church they made a meal of me,

ripe fig even the starved birds would pluck & eat:
beak to beak & lip & eye & I, bone-shattered –

vermillion brilliant.
To Them I was never essential,

a voice whispering in the depths of a desert
convincing you I am something else –

Woman, Teacher,
Heathen, Witch,

blood-jet of the God-vessel
nailed out of His right mind.

It was not me, I had nothing to do with it:
The shards of the Parabalani fly like planets.

Each slice of slate, the stars hurtle closer.
Where is your Walker On Water?

I do not see Him,
He is not here.

Above me: silver bodies,
all those gold-spun suns.

I take them into me:
here is my blood on the stones –

I give it to Them.
My last breaths merely wind,

my riven blood
water –

Opening slice by slice:
the Heavens –

Celestial:
I rise & rise –

unto –
until:

Bucha

You have to remember, at some point
someone was taking butter out of a butter dish
when the windows blew in –

& perhaps it was fine china,
then suddenly it was bricks –
smoke, fire, human bone.

& then a child or dog
screaming.
It became rubble,

it became twenty-three
-year-olds wielding Kalashnikovs.
It became necessary.

You Google: *How do you make
the perfect Molotov cocktail?*
Shaken, lit, but not stirred.

It became a tank rolling over
a civilian's car & children pulled
close to burning from a missile-hot building

& running, scattering along a street
under gunfire to what?
Mass graves dug by Russian soldiers?

It became bunkers
& lone dogs barking & all of us watching
screen by screen. There are bodies

splayed on streets where they ran –
though no one comes to claim them:
smoke bombing itself into sky

resembling a treeline
where (once upon a time)
trees used to be –

& now there is no real end to this poem

Sweetbread

The man holding the phone & filming says
They're sending these kids to war like pieces of meat –
while the young Russian cries & tries to stay upright.

He's sipping tea in sunlight, his hands shaking.
No-one really knows why he's there to begin with –
& he's twenty if he's a day.

Hungry for days, downing burning tea
from Ukrainians as if it's God's own juice
a pie in his hand he doesn't remember how to eat.

How much has he been spat at
after being told it was a routine exercise
& not a fucking war,

packed off, gun in hand,
to starve & thirst & beg for mercy
before the faces of those you're invading?

A Ukrainian girl has called his mother in a fucking car park,
of all places, this Russian woman she has never met – the girl tells his mother:
Natasha, everything's alright, he's safe, someone will contact you!

A Ukrainian man in the background says
They don't even know where they're going,
they're going by old maps.

The girl reassures his mother in Russia,
she tells her *God bless! Here, Natasha, please talk to him. Speak to your son.*
The boy is trying not to cry before the face of his mother.

His suddenly young face
overcome by confusion & their mercy,
buried in his collar. People his colleagues have shot

or bombed. This is the place
where shame lies: discovering the lie as a lie,
you bury your chin in your collar.

You go as deep into yourself as you can.
You hedgehog, close up.
You sip tea & thank your captors.

His 'captor' tells this boy's mother:
He's healthy. He's okay, we're feeding him –
while he nods in a car park, forgetting how to eat.

She strokes the back of his head.
She is teaching him to relax in a way
she hasn't since the war started.

Far off, bombs disperse
over a line of low-hanging sun,
artillery, tanks & she's telling Natasha he has eaten.

Whole cities shouting in the faces of invaders,
the future unravelling forward,
blast by blast.

The Shroud of David

Now there are guns
& an unmaking of borders –
& though people speak of death

as if it is a thing that happens
only outwardly: because they cannot voice
the absence of the one who made it

but will not come again, feeling
useless – like Persephone doing
& undoing a death-shroud she shall never complete –

because what else is there
but to shroud your whole self?
Let the Magdalene weep

in her eternity of marble,
& the Virgin smile sweetly out
under her veils of purity.

Take your God-wafers,
your holy waters,
your vats of Christ-blood wine.

Those are stones, but
we are essential –
a voice in a wilderness,

a serpent
hissing
in a Russian tree.

No Man's Empire

*after last letters written by Irish rebels executed by the occupational forces
(British firing squad) at Kilmainham Gaol. Dublin, Easter 1916.*

There is a drop panel in the room,
but they tell me I am not destined for it.

I will be brought out
bound & blindfolded.
The Empire will name me 'Traitor'.

This Country is no man's empire.

It is a cold yard,
I have heard shots all morning –

but they have given me pen & paper.
I am ready to die –

The one bitterness that death has for me
is the separation it brings.

I counted the cost of this
& am ready to pay it.
Mother –

your dear self.
They have given me a priest
& I am ready to go.

O Holy
Mother of God –
below

there is the door
out to the yard –

I hear footsteps –

P.S. *I understand that the German expedition*
which I was counting on actually set sail
but was defeated by the British.

I must go now.

I have no more time.
When you hear my name & the shots

kiss Kitty for me.
Your Loving Son,

Bog Man in a Museum

after Old Croghan Man, *a possible sacrificial prince of the Iron Age.*

Cut
straight through the heart:
this is a sacrifice.

Peat, bog-oak,
stringent hands bound
together, tarred.

Necklace of rope, arrowhead of shale
& a wan mouth at its last moment
pouring open to mirror sky.

No silver bracelets could save you,
a bad harvest
& some King's son must die.

What of the child, crying at night,
the mother-princess?
Who awaits something –

sunrise,
footsteps
on snow?

How the mountains shifted
& the glacier – glassy in its own element
settled over the body.

This is betrayal: the body's & nature's –
it is not mine.
I cannot take it.

Yet, his mouth, tarred, twisted –
poured open to sky
is a largess, a trifle conceding nothing.

Even here,
in this rarefied room,
air motes float

in their faint regalia –
white saints falling through air
surely & whitely.

The body turf-bound,
stricken –
& the mouth,

the colour of it?
& how the mouth begs
Carry it, carry it.

The Golden Hour

Once we had days & days
of the sea the shade of green tourmaline,
        stretching out away from us.
        The sands dusting our ankles
whenever you could steal away from the bar
when no one would notice.

Once we had days & days
of your hand in mine, behind their backs.
        Small touches, a hand on a hip, maybe.
        Or your fingertips tracing the line of my bare shoulders
when no-one was watching.

        I don't know what I thought,
but I thought,
Maybe this is?

     ★

The last time I saw you:
        the breeze full of orange blossom,
        you, standing in sun – in haze –
        out in the middle of a road, in Crete.
        A dishrag hurriedly slung over one shoulder
& a hand clamped to the soft nest of hair
at the back of your head.

        & I thought,
        I have lovingly held that head.
I have lovingly tussled that nest of hair.
        You couldn't see me,
        though from the car I saw you waving.
        I can't tell you –
that expression haunts me still:
not a smile, not sadness,
exactly –
        something else
& for twenty-five years

I have failed to find the right word,
      the *right* way to describe it –
maybe it's the dishcloth that slid
off your shoulder,
unnoticed?

      How naturally
      it came to lie there, as if it had always been there,
there –
at your feet, in the heat & dry dust:

      As if the heart-lost man in that golden hour,
      utterly broken
in the hot street,
wavering & waving,
      bore it no consequence.

The heart is an abscess
waiting   to burst –

Io, Transformed into a Cow, is Handed to Juno by Jupiter

after the painting by David Tenier the Elder, 1638.

I.

Jupiter Attempts to Lie to Juno

But what will you do with it?
It is true, the beast is a terrible beauty.
The blonde hair of its fine, high flanks, the sensuous muscularity
that begs the hand to smooth it, the mouth to water,
lips to moisten, or to part.

I confess, love, I was undone –
I craved the creature for myself.

II.

Juno Curses Io

I could kill it. He would not dare to stop me –
or expose his lie – if I ripped the knife from ear to ear.

Look at it, so pathetic,
stood there like that: doe-eyed & twitching
before me, the mouth accosting itself –
caught in the act.

I think it blushes. I bet, at night,
it touches itself at the thought of him,
his thighs, his hands, the hair that curls a spiral at his navel –
I cannot allow it.

At my word a gadfly flies, its mouth malicious,
starved & delirious over the waters of Egypt,
delicious in its bloodlust –
This is my gift, a life in endless threat.

Make a home here, Io, under foreign stars.
See the moon rising over the Nile, the crocodiles
& their song; a razor-silver nocturne played to blood –
their teeth at night.

III.

Juno Warns Io

I have given you magnanimity. It will not come again.
Re-take your skin, but here strip: unloose yourself
of notions, of all ties that bind his pull upon you –

for I am the pestle & the mortar, & when you are dust
there will still be only me & me

& old Invidia –
her ancient shadow passing
lightly upon a wall.

IV.

Juno Contemplates Forgiveness

Is it within me to forgive him this?
Search the stars their white hot bastardies
that I could find benevolence to bend again before him,
unfurl my deepest velvet darks & gift to him
a token, totem, sign of trust –

like Helios, at the final moment,
gifting Heracles a guilty freedom –
the golden bowl?

Strange Husbandry

Your phone is a mystery, an abyss
on whose surface one name in particular

swims up from the depths every darkness –
like some gaping, terrible fish.

Drifting into your inbox night after night,
glittering your darks like a masochist, mouth glistening

for the upturned curve of a sharpened tip,
the hook, the hook, the hook –

How intimate was he? Was it 'biblical'? A serial thing?
Or a name-only, spit–in–the–face, pump–fuck affair?

The sweet lip-rip & cum-in-me-bro,
the bants, the bants, the bants –

the still fresh memory of his groan
& glisten in the hot August night last summer.

I can't understand it.
I have killed all my lovers,

tasted the dripping iniquity of my exes.
Old bones I have licked & discarded.

Why do you keep him?
It is such strange husbandry –

poor animal leashed & breathless,
begging for lashing,

for the smack on skin,
the sex-scent of leather.

His last, best ass-tickler. In the deep breath of evening
I hear him buzzing, blue-bottle fly, fetid & pestering over your Insta,

sticky feelers inking his own dark void in a frenzy –
dying for a sweetness, for a skin-on-skin lick of you.

Heart-eyes on your stories, on post after post.
Let's be honest, it is cruel –

letting him keep at it like this.
I say we bag him – blind kitten. Runt. It is futile.

Let there be no idols before me
for I am the Love, your Dog.

I am a mouthful of such sweet god –
your holy confirmation of holes.

Unlike him
I see only you & you:

sole idol for whose presence
the waves I shear & part:

O Exodus – how slow, how steady
you tear apart the last fine strings,

the gut-belly wrench
to the sweet, red-ripped centre

to the last wet heart,
Love, you will enter,

enter.
Enter.

Circe on Æа

I will be the sea — as the Aegean
salting its indigoes before me.

I am the action
& the word at once.

What is it that was seen in me?
Somehow, there is a justice in this:

they say men scream like babies
when the jugular is jagged.

First they are turned to pig
& eaten after.

I have never been so flush of blood.
Take it from one who knows:

the meat—juice pinkens & sluices
if you salt the skin.

Listen for the sweet—crisp, the crackle.
They come to me, wielding mouths

of sweetmeats, these lucent plums:
these tongues I will jelly & eat, berry-sweetened.

It's so easy to entrance them
it is almost sickening.

All you need is a wish & a smile,
a finger willing them closer.

They never see the fire sparking
in the quiet, darkened distance —

lit like the frail, thin
line of a fate not worth knowing.

I whisper only of sweet things, their potential,
of the many stickied candies

they will yet grow
& become.

Tear In Your Hand

after the Tori Amos song.

Gold flakes: light in morning
catching between birdcall & curtain.

Silence – one person waking –
faces another person waking.
We blink a little

& die a little each time
& every touch
means only
Hello.

Your hand pulling my hips onward
toward your hips, your lips
on my lips

in such bright need,
you shine:
face intolerable –

we strip, become juiced,
flesh-laden, mercied,
at need –

& by end
you might say
become *othered* –

Salomé

...that red-ripped, cloven skin:
& the veins slivered over
a bare stone floor fit for a King.

The fresh, cold plate
like a destiny
& his screams so silver:

the plate a mirror
of horrors – so solidified, desired.
To my mother's house

swiftly I come –
my fingers red. I stare & stare
at them: they are foreigners –

to the guards
I said: *Red* –
from berry–picking.

Time Lapse at Porthmeor

We haven't yet developed bad habits.

The wind is lapping the surf like a dog.

The five of us are watching the sun set over the sea.

In the soft, dark cloak of night we will uncork the wine.

Your huge hands are tender, warm on my shoulders.

Around us, the others take turns rolling dice.

Beyond the open window, the sea will be salting the rockpools into the deep dawn hours.

I don't mind telling you, you're developing a habit of holding my hand while you sleep.

Deep, dark crevices, my hands keep reaching.

We climb & climb, boots slipping, wet stone.

Sheer rock face – I sweep the moss off wet stone.

Boots slipping, I go & go –

You reaching back & back.

Natural Chemistry

The doctors disagree on what's wrong with me.
One denounces my medication –
incredulous I'm alive.

No cardiac arrhythmia? Palpitations?
No respiratory distress & you've been drinking, moderately?

Even my blood pressure is normal.
He finds it difficult to believe.
Outside, somewhere,

my friends pick apart the platter of saucy details
that is my illness over cocktails.

The voices have stopped, they are silent.
The grasses no longer whisper to me of their immortality,
the verdant beauty of the bladed edge I shall never achieve.

By morning I rattle along
the walls of my brain, empty.

My oesophagus a dried–up riverbed,
& eyes like two stones turning
on walls, on streets, on grimaces or familiar faces.

A bus broke a red light the other day.
At the moment it would've hit me, I stopped short.

The man next to me startled
but I didn't even flinch.
I lit a cigarette.

They tell me
This is what normal feels like.

By night
I'm a pill bottle,
slowly digesting itself.

Putting the Damage On

after the song by Tori Amos

I am no longer really sleeping.
But how do you catch a moving threshold?

There is so much to see
under the tin shade of stars –

a fox chases the ghost of its want
down the street.

Night changes
everything.

How brilliant
the night breaks open,

the moon fondly silvers my hair –
the ash tree rustles its leaves in comfort.

You take to handing me my pills at sunset.
They do nothing but burn

in the fire of my blood.
I dream while awake.

I am humming & trembling –
the world burns vivid & tactile.

Everything holds some erotic detail –
the bend of the lamp, whorls on a tabletop.

Your red rub delicately
over your tongue.

The soft warmth of your hands offering
sedatives to the chatter of my mouth.

The Descent from the Cross

after the painting by Rembrandt (studio of), 1634.

I.

Night falls over Golgotha.
Under a blood moon we work by lit lamp –
the hills still, quiet

except for the hum of women:
a low weeping
& the men at work over a body

the soul left.

I, Magdalena, (stone-silent),
lay the shroud that shall hold the body.

I take the veil from my hair
& cover his.

II.

What holds the body,
if not hands?

What do hands do with tenderness
when the body refuses to hold it?

What should I do with these hands –
these wounds of God –

but hold them?

Does it matter if they know
they are implements –

divine or otherwise?

III.

The gates of Jerusalem flower in darkness:
our small band hastening on with our cart.

The soldiers at the gate fall silent —
we flank the body
veiled in fine cloth.

I walk with the first rank of women
into the city. Even at this hour
there are crowds.

Beneath my hand,
through the thin white linen,

I feel his hair.

Though it has been days,
death has not limpened it.

I feel the softness of his curls still.

IV.

Nicodemus brought vats
of myrrh & aloe, befitting a king –

paid, he said,
of his own pocket.

The women work washing the body
of grime, of dust from the hill.

We work at wiping
death from the body.

I tend to the small mercy:
the wound in the side.

I cannot take my eyes from the face –
as though it were sleeping.

I cannot find the sufferance my eyes have seen.
I cannot find pain, as when the voice cried out

& then was gone. In the ninth hour,
on that ghastly hill, that voice.

The voice that quieted
my needle working on the shroud,

that raised my eyes
& brought my hand to still.

V.

The knocking so astounded,
& the servant who brought him,

ashen, to the House of Joseph –
the same Centurion.

I must speak my mind – my hand,
it acted out of mercy. I ask forgiveness.

Nicodemus took the fine-wrapped gift.

We unwrapped the cloth:
a spearhead –

& the blood,
still partly wet.

Our eyes in low light
glanced amongst ourselves
& glistened.

VI.

What is left to be said of the empty tomb
or the rock before my eyes rolled back?
Or of the hill

where wind alone
ate breaths
out of the dying brood?

It is a hill of bones.

We sail on quiet water,
the sailors about their work.
They do not know me, or don't say.

I veil my hair.
Even the children are quieted.

All is memory, impartial,
unclear –

But I have scented my wrists
with aloe & with myrrh.

VII.

The red moon whitened.

Here, the horizon breaks its yolk, dripping
a dawn-flush morning after morning.

This sea is a shroud
& I glisten it.

Our roaming days crack the world open, oar by oar.
I have braided a lock of your hair into mine.

The veil shifts in the wind, my fingers find
a thread of you tied to me still.

O Galilee, my Galilee –
it will be night there now.

Your hair threaded to mine, I will take you;
beloved, I will carry you –

I will carry you
to the end of the world.

The Disappearing Woman

I.

Missing, they say: *No trace.*
& for weeks we turn over the park,

the nearby farms, the fields.
Everywhere close to anywhere.

Eventually there were plates to wash,
kids to dress & each morning

we searched & searched silos, barns,
cornfields – we bent their full, dull, gold heads –

& far fields, car trunks,
sheds – anything we could & for a while

it felt like every blade of grass knew a thing we didn't
& we couldn't sleep or move

& eventually the river kept on being a river
& every man looked like danger

II.

Boys walked girls to school in twos & twos.
Still there are far fields, the whitened silence of grass

blades each winter & here a river & how
year after year

the spring falls like a drunk,
giving us nothing over & over.

& the river just slides over itself
slick like it knows nothing.

& all of us stand here pissed off
swearing, wishing maybe,

if it all flowed the *right* way,
it could wash all this bullshit the flying fuck away.

Silent.
Slipshod, the river.

A Poem in the Voice of My Dead Uncle

My heart is learning to be a butterfly.
Like a small boy,

it practices every day –
it wants to be a man.

So, one day, it will teach itself
to leave me.

& it will learn, like every man,
what it is to be a forest:

to be a sea of branches –
a still, silent ocean.

& it will learn silence:
such sweet

purple
the colour of rage.

Gun Country

I.

They say you die once –
though I have also heard it told,

as any goodwife knows, you die
the final time your name is spoken.

Tell me
which plant or tree,

or three, outlasts us?
Ash, Oak or Evergreen?

Or a Hawthorn, let it be
a Hawthorn –

under which everything's buried
but anything grows.

Witch Hazel, Witch Hazel –
which everyone knows.

II.

That was the year I shot the pheasant –
corn shot through with blood

& blood so we couldn't chew
kernels from the stalks that day.

I bruised a shoulder,
but I got a clean shot

& a blue-green metaled feather:
a good clean country-boy killing,

thorns stuck bowl-edged
or bottom-swimming.

The meat:
the shots in it.

An Bhean Sí / The Banshee

I am almost nothing.

There is dew on the berries,
little frosted suicides
dissolving in a drop.

I am the thing that takes & takes,
always giving & receiving.
Love is an abstract thing.

I cry for the loss of it. I cry for the glance
you probably give him
on a Saturday morning naked, in bed,

in pure shone light –
is it my face rising with the moon
in a cold kitchen?

This lit room in which
I have placed the plates, the glasses,
your pots, our pans. Tell me,

do you rest well knowing
that new animal breathes
in the same bed my breath gave out?

How well fed do you keep him?
These fields are fogged & deep.
Mist

& how mist moves,
a smoke-like kind of
memory.

The Astrology of Trees

for Sinéad

I.

The sun inhabits itself –
selfish, loping, blindly
staggering only to sink
on the lips of its own horizon,

a sky of hammered metal.
Bruised as any hard-loved lover.
It is nothing I recognise.

It is not my sky I am flying through.
I have thirteen hundred

pounds to my name.
I have my suitcase, my books, a journal.
I have my name –

& they will all twist it, licking,
under tumbling tongues.

II.

Who was that boy on the ward,
his pale face restless with energy?
Watching the conifers green & green –
unsure toes tipping over
the tripwire to death?

I do not know him.
I have left him back there.
That was not my life,
it was someone else's.

Do not cover the paintings in my room,
leave my books to gather dust

just as they are.

Do not sheet the mirrors:
it is not final.

III.

Moons rise & set.
Days roll their dulled heads.

London settles itself
within me, the streets begin
to know my feet
& the underground wind
whistles only to me,

it seems.
The skateboarders,
the buskers & lights

along the Southbank at night –
slowly, I have begun to refer to it as
'home'. The leaves come & go.

It is not my home.

IV.

It will almost be winter there now.
In the distance there will be snow

on the tops of mountains. I know
the river will be swelling its banks.
Frost on the rails of the bridge out of town

& the motorway stretching out: all amber lights
& signposts & nowhere to go.

I rise at dawn here. Fog settles in hills,
a laden garden, the Cherry Blossoms –
how they loom out monstrous.

Your voice on the phone tells me
It's just life – just as usual...

& yet, year by year, sister, over the wild, wild
heads of trees, the sun's pale seasons weaken.

"Louise, No Matter What Happens, I'm Glad I Came with You"

for the Louise to my Thelma

How about lunch? my mother says, suddenly.
She throws a spatula into the kitchen sink.

It *thunks* because she throws it:
she's done.

To me it seems unusual – she's classy,
& this is just blunt. Surprising:

the sinks thrums & throws up bubbles.
I am fourteen years old.

I look out the window
she's been looking out of:

our dog is licking poisonous
flowers that called for a vet visit last week.

Neither of us speak. We watch her eat them.
We know she'll get sick

& stop it. She's done it before.
She is tired beyond belief.

I am also tired – *Do I need a bag?*
I am feeling reckless.

She says: *We're just going for lunch but don't tell anybody.*
It's just you & me.

We drive for over an hour,
enter the next county over.

The lamb at lunch is delicious.
Between us we have twenty missed calls.

We scream *The Sidewinder Sleeps Tonite* out the car windows
like they'd take music away tomorrow.

You alright Thelma?
I'm smokin' cigarettes! I yell out an open window

blowing air out my fingers, half Carlow
& Kildare flying by blank-eyed sheep –

This machine can only swallow money...
Darkening sky & amber lights on a highway –

how the way back home formed
into a thing again: a spatula slick & soaped,

floating face-up in a dead pool of water.
Like a sink stopper, still,

dull, reeling for
a faint breath of air.

Piece Designed by the Artist to be Incomplete:

after the death of Elizabeth Wurtzel

These blank spaces: liminal
like birdcall, fog

smoking over
a bridge.

This is a thing
that has happened.

These steps: wide
vagary toward spaces

like some odd distance –
like cows bellowing in

the shroud of an Irish field,
as a thing un-ending

but knitting, let's say,
a kitchen in which

someone puts a kettle on:
so there is tea

& dogs barking
as if –

:*"As If"* – Conjunction:
Definition: Miriam-Webster Dictionary:

–1: as it would be if It was as *if* he had lost his last friend.
–3: that It seemed as *if* the day would never end.

You never did text me back & I didn't
want to bother you.

The gods barked.
So we prayed to the dogs.

Someone in fog – in field –
shrouded a kettle & filled it

over & over again –
cows bellowed a vagary

of tea thin as birdcall –
liminal:

like a backdoor
hung open –

hung open,
almost as if –

The Next New Testament

for Leo

will be written of sand and shadow.
There will be smoke in the air
and Andrew Christian underwear on the floor

drenched, slovenly, on a Sunday
afternoon around about the time
church starts.

One of us will be cleaning ourselves off
glistening/sticky/in pure wet love
with each other, our male form –

whistling whilst we gather bathrobes/coffee/
birds chattering/the constant squirrel
burying his bits in the soft soil at the hedge

in the depths of the garden, in the house you will soon leave.
The moons that rises over this house will not remember you.
At Limehouse

the moon will move through a room,
ceilings three and a half metres tall/sash windows/
shoes inside the door –

flowers will drink from a fine crystal vase.
And everything drooping and leaking,
hanging/heavy/heavenly.

The next New Testament will be written
by men loving men/foot-sure/even. Fine-footed
and drinking out of fine crystal/in love

with each other/
our male forms –
heavy-swung/heavenly.

What I cannot know now
is my absence
there.

Acknowledgements

This collection was written over four years – years which have spanned a global pandemic, a new war in Europe and a vast change in the societal structure globally, both in terms of work culture and also how we as an international community view ourselves and interact. Thank you to anyone who has worked to keep us all safe during any of this. Our global debt to your is insurmountable.

First, I thank my sister, Sinéad. She believed in me first. I showed her my first poems before anyone else and she was a whole world away.

I want to thank Crystal Stone for being one of my best friends & my constant critic during the creation of this collection – *Gurl, you are, and will always be, a global phenomenon!*

Chen Chen has spent literal years boosting my confidence in a way no one would probably bother if I was an actual, total asshole so he really is one of the nicest people you could call a friend, especially if you're a poet.

Richie Hofmann is always thoughtful, lovely and a good ear when we both remember to talk to each other. Richie, you're a gem.

Blas Falconer: I cannot ever repay your time, my friend, for your kindness and your very acute advice to me over several years. You are my mentor in so many ways and I hope my work reflects it and does you proud, even a little. I always, always hear your voice telling me in each poem I write: "Less is always more."

Peter LaBerge – thank you, thank you, thank you. You are a star. You have always been kind. You're a gentleman.

Kailey Tedesco I cannot thank enough, enough, enough. You witchy witch woman. Hecate kisses.

John Compton, Paul Ian Cross, Louis Spencer, Alessandro Brusa, Sarah Howe, Jack Warren, Mag Gabbart, Patrick Kindig – you're all awesome and hello my lovelies!

Leonardo Maugeri: I cannot say a thing to you that I have not already written privately nor said aloud, you are the best friend a man could ask for. I don't know what to say except to quote Anna Akhmatova:

"Light months will fly over us
like snowy stars."
There are some mountains which cannot be moved.

Paulo Morini, Eleonora Sammartino, Alessandro & Stefano, Daniela, Shereen – hello, you two fabulous creatures! – Danila & Tim, Ellen & Rob, Florian, Valentina (and her many fabulous dinners! Yes, that's a hint), Maria & Alex, Elisa, Ilaria, Giulia, Francesca, Marta, Marzia, Martina, et. al: I love the past awful years of a global pandemic and all the rest of it because it introduced me to all of you.

Silvana, Conceto, Novella, Vincenzo, Raffa & little Stefano – thank you so much for your sweetness, your hospitality and your immense kindness. I love you all like family and my thanks could not be greater. Can–Can promises lots of balloons. Let's always have balloons. I will keep posting more. Mi dispiace Novi è Vincenzo.

Caralyn de Cambra, Dani Blue, Rob Hartnett, Robby, Liv, Dariusz, David H, David McD, Nat, Cat, Alice and Jonny, Chiara, Siobhán, Alex, Vanessa the Fabulous, Joyce, Jeff, Andrew Davis and of course Matt – *El Pellarojo* – much love.

Laura-Mai O'Reilly has been constant since I was about four years old. Lozzie: you are my fucking soulmate. I will be here for you forever; you have my whole damn heart. Do you have that No. 9 acrylic? Look – I put it in your bag! And I did not lose my index finger, it *broke off*.

Bróna Malcolm – do I need to say anything? I love you whole heartedly like a sister. I love Conor like a sister too, but like, in a man way.

My family are the bright lights of my life. Mam, Dad, Sinéad, Dave, Oisín, Diarmuid, Caoimhe, Aoife – my heart, my breath. Nothing I could ever say to any of you would be enough, nor cover how huge my love is for any of you. You have made me believe in love as a power source in itself, in myself as a person and in the ability of working toward anything to produce a result. You're the source of everything in me that is strong.

Justine, David, Trish (and Richard) – love, love and more love (and love). Imagine how much poorer our lives would be if we hadn't been curious enough to ask questions? We have an insane family history – I wouldn't have it any other way, because it has given me you guys!

Virginia –*Lady Peck*– you know I adore the ground you walk on, and it is never near enough. It is never, ever near enough.

Marie Nolan, Sharon, Lloyd – I love, love, love you. More than most. I'm with you guys every time I'm socialising and you're not there, but I always wish you were.

Ruslan Fedasyuk – I hope in some small way I make you proud with some of these poems. Mostly I'm glad you're safe, Rusty, with a family who loves you and you're taking care of, like you wanted. Love you, man.

Brian, Paul, Matusko, and Bella (please make another horror movie set in Scotland, I beg you. One is not enough for my whole life. I will even hold a boom, I'll do anything as a background actor if you'll just do it – I mean this very seriously!), Viktor, Twig, Lydia, Shelley (gang of gangs!) – thank you. Samuel Parnell: I love you, man. I will always, always have your back. Every single time. I would give you the shirt off my back. Always. You're my dude. If there's ever a zombie apocalypse, we're doing it, the two of us.

Special, loveable, mention goes out to my loves: Christine Monahan (and YES Georgina, you too! I love you also, don't get jealous), Aoife and Emer. We are far apart, sure, and I'm absolutely rubbish at being in touch, but I love you.

I will forget people, forgive me – thank you all for being lights on a runway with an unknown fucking destination and no air–traffic controller. You are the best of the best of people.

To the late, great Elizabeth Wurtzel: they say never meet your heroes, but I refute that. Several times over. Doesn't matter, you're gone but you're fabulous. I'm sorry we didn't get to swap books. You taught to me to give absolutely zero fucks given. And you know something? I no longer have change.

To the editors and staff readers of all the magazines and journals which have published not just these poems, but any of my poems, thank you so much for time, effort and appreciation. It is a long, taxing and thankless (but ultimately rewarding) job, as I well know from four years of *Anomaly Literary Journal,* and my thanks are given very humbly for it.

Thank you to the following journals for including work from this collection:

71

'Hypatia' – Ghost City Review | 2024
'Io, Transformed into a Cow is Handed to Juno by Jupiter'
'Piece Designed by the Artist to Be Incomplete: After the death of Elizabeth Wurtzel'
'Bucha'
'The Next New Testament' – The Tomahawk Creek Review | 2023

'The Descent from the Cross' & 'August' – Letters Journal | February 2023

'Salomé' – The Rush | August 2022

'Circe on Æaea' – Grim & Gilded | 2002

'Strange Husbandry' – Progenitor Art & Literary Journal | Forthcoming 2022

'The Disappearing Woman' – New Writing Scotland | Summer 2021.

'A Poem in the Voice of My Dead Uncle' – Poet Lore | Fall/Winter 2020.

'Lockdown' & 'Witch's Means' – Stirring: A Literary Collection, Vol. 23, Ed. 1, | Winter 2020.

'The Golden Hour' – Connecticut River Review | 2020.

'Hazmat' – Northern New England Review, & also, Snapdragon: a Journal of Art & Healing, as well as being featured in the Bologna in Lettere 2020 Festival | 2020.

'Bog Man in a Museum' – Cardinal Sins | Fall 2016.

Thank you to my fabulous editors Rhian Edwards and Zoë Brigley. I don't know what to say – who on earth in their right mind would love this collection? Or fight for it? You are both incredible writers. You have taken such great care, such love and been there each step of the way no matter how dumb any question I ever asked was.

Who could ask for better editors, as a poet, than two fabulous poets? Thank you you both so much for everything you do.

We all engage in a bit of *Strange Husbandry* in life, an odd way of managing our resources, however you interpret 'resources'.

Further Notes

'Witch's Means'

Giles Corey was an English colonialist accused of witchcraft in 1692 and pressed to death by boulders. For this series of trials, he became a martyr of people improperly tried and executed.

'Bog Man in a Museum'

Old Croghan Man, or *Seanfhear Chruacháin*, in the Irish language, is a well-preserved Irish Iron–Age 'bog body' found in June 2003. His remains are kept on display at the Irish Museum of Archaeology. He is believed to have died between 362 BCE & 175 BCE, making the body over 2,000 years old. He was likely in his early twenties when he died. His stomach indicated a recent diet of buttermilk & wheat & four months prior to his death led a highly meat–rich diet. Due to the change in his diet, we might assume he knew he would be sacrificed, or executed — history indicates as a failure of the ruling royal family. His nipples were cut, which from this time period indicates a lack of confidence in the leadership of the King & his descendants. It is an act of emasculation. He had manicured nails which suggests he was not used to manual labour. He was decapitated & his body was cut in half. He also bore an injury to one arm, evidence that he tried to defend himself. It is clear he fought against his own destruction. If you go visit him in the museum, do say hello from me. I know him very well.

'No Man's Empire'

The italics in this poem are real words written by men executed at Kilmainham Gaol by firing squad, under the end of 800 years of British occupation of Ireland during Easter 1916. The text in this poem that is not in italics is, of course, poetic license.

'The Shroud of David'

On March 6th, 2022, on the birthdate of Michelangelo, the city mayor of Firenze, Dario Nardella, shrouded the replica statue of David, in Piazza della Signoria under black cloth, to honour Ukraine's lost citizens.

'The Descent from the Cross'

The poem is based on the painting of the same title & is narrated in the voice of the finely dressed woman in red, portrayed on the lowest left–hand corner of Rembrant's imagining, whom I've imagined to be

Mary Magdalene. It details The Descent – as she experiences it – but also her personal love & affection for the man himself, whatever the status of his 'being', the cleansing of the body, & finally her departure from Galilee (and the historical record – such as it is) as a whole. Unlike every other person in this painting, the woman in red is significant: unlike any other character painted in this work, for circa 1634, she is dressed in entirely contemporary clothing for the time – that of an upper middle class Amsterdam housewife of means. For contemporary audiences this may have had an effect akin to painting a punk rocker into a renaissance painting – it leaves little to the imagination that despite the situation the painting illustrates, she may, I like to think, have been its true subject.